W9-DFN-338

JNF

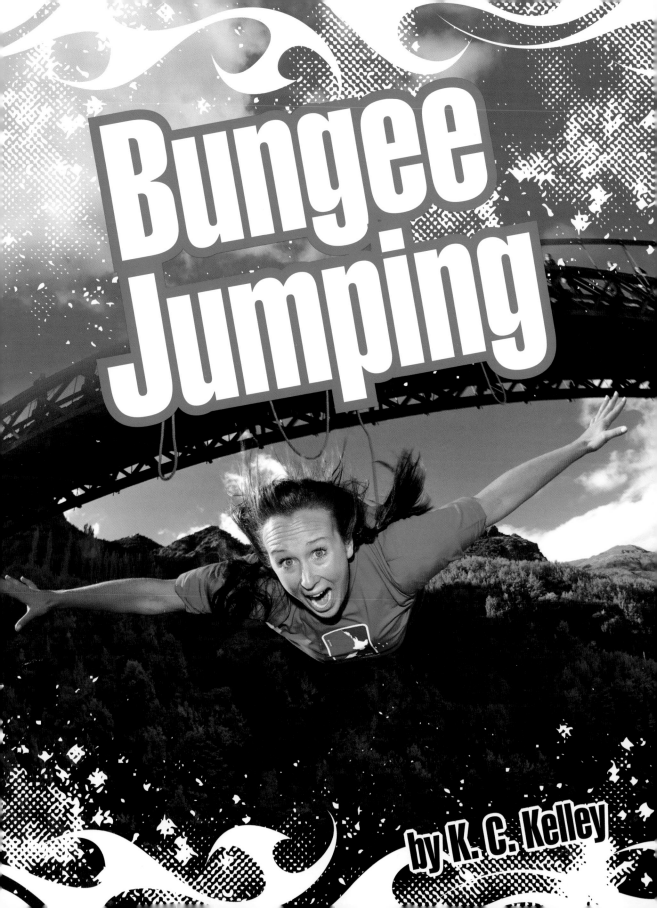

Bungee Jumping

by K. C. Kelley

Published by The Child's World®
1980 Lookout Drive
Mankato, MN 56003-1705
800-599-READ
www.childsworld.com

The Child's World®: Mary Berendes, Publishing Director
Shoreline Publishing Group, LLC: James Buckley Jr.,
    Production Director
The Design Lab: Design and production

ISBN: 978-1-60973-206-6
LCCN: 2011928883

Photo credits: Cover: Courtesy AJ Hackett Bungy/
New Zeland. Interior: AJ Hackett Bungy/New Zealand:
8; AP/Wide World: 12, 20 Corbis: 7; dreamstime.com:
Sanderni: 4, Jan Kranendonk: 16, Phil Berry: 24; iStock:
19, 23, 27, 28; Photos.com: 11, 15.

Printed in the United States of America
Mankato, Minnesota
July, 2011
PA02094

Table of Contents

The head-down dive is a popular way to bungee jump.

CHAPTER ONE

What Goes Down . . . Must Come Up!

Suddenly, the chase came to a quick end. The man had raced away from the enemy for a long time, but they had caught up. Breathless, he stood atop a super-high dam. The enemy slowly moved forward. There was only one way out for the hero: down.

The hero stepped to the edge and jumped!

Down . . . down . . . down he plunged! Then, with a sudden *boing*, he stopped falling . . . and started bouncing back up! He had escaped the enemy!

This amazing jump was very real . . . but it was in a movie. **Stunt man** Wayne Michaels had just made the highest bungee jump ever—more than 720 feet (220 m). His leap came from the top of the Verzasca Dam in Switzerland. In 2002, this jump, for the James Bond movie *GoldenEye*, was voted the best movie stunt ever.

Wayne's stunt was another amazing part of the story of bungee jumping. People doing this extreme sport jump from high places. They are tied to very stretchy bungee cords. The cords turn the people into a kind of yo-yo, bouncing up and down at the bottom of their jumps.

Though bungee jumping uses the latest type of cords for safety, it's actually a very old activity. People living in the village of Bunlap on the South Pacific island of Vanuatu were the first. For centuries, they have done land diving. Divers climb a tall tower. They tie **lianas**, or long vines, to their ankles. Then they jump. The vines stretch and catch the jumpers just before they hit the ground.

First they built a tower on Bunlap . . .
then they jumped off it.

The bungee site Hackett opened is still
thrilling visitors like this jumper.

Some students in England were inspired by the folks in Bunlap. In 1979, the Oxford University Dangerous Sports Club made the first jumps using bungee cords. They were arrested for jumping without permission! The club kept jumping, however. Later, they jumped off the Golden Gate Bridge in San Francisco and the Royal Gorge Bridge in Colorado.

In 1987, a daredevil named A.J. Hackett jumped off the Eiffel Tower in Paris. Hackett became another bungee **pioneer**. In his home country of New Zealand, he opened the first place for anyone to try this sport. Soon people from all over were leaping from Hackett's bridge . . . and bouncing back up!

Bungee jumping soon became popular among people looking for a safe thrill—mostly safe, that is. There were some accidents. However, most places where people can jump are carefully run. Bungee jumping is now found in dozens of countries around the world. Some jumpers make trips to new places just to try out bungee sites.

Bungee jumpers know that what goes down . . . must come up.

This bungee site is a platform
hanging from a crane.

The black straps on this jumper are the harness.
Ankle straps give extra support.

CHAPTER TWO

Bungee Basics

Two pieces of gear are key to bungee jumping. The first is the **harness**. This is a series of straps, ropes, and cords that attach the bungee cords to a person. Most people wear a harness attached to their ankles. Other harnesses strap around the chest.

The other key pieces of gear are the bungee cords themselves. Bungee cords are long strands of rubber wrapped with **nylon** or cotton. The cords used by jumpers were first created for use in the military.

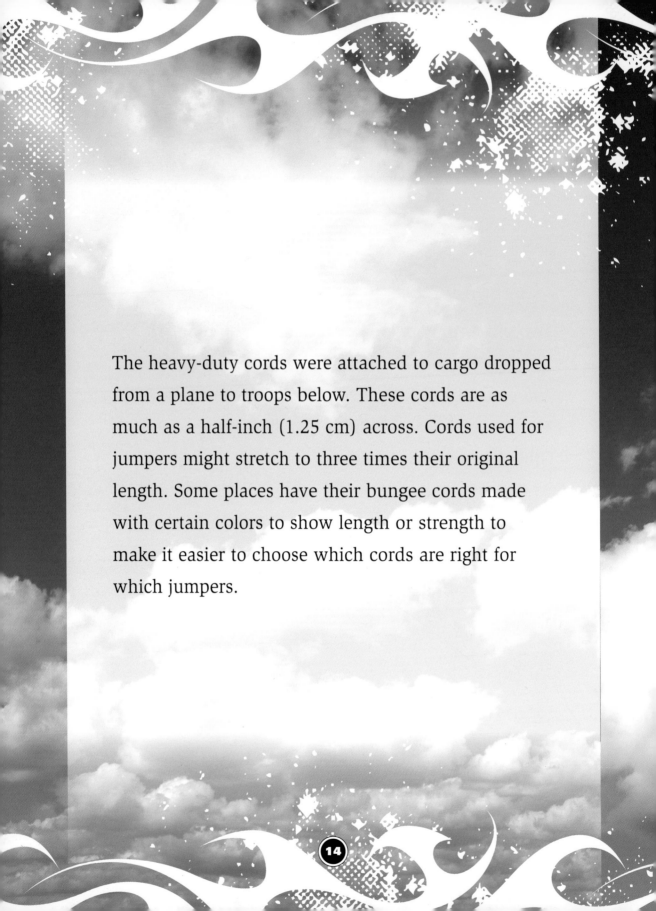

The heavy-duty cords were attached to cargo dropped from a plane to troops below. These cords are as much as a half-inch (1.25 cm) across. Cords used for jumpers might stretch to three times their original length. Some places have their bungee cords made with certain colors to show length or strength to make it easier to choose which cords are right for which jumpers.

Down and down . . . the bungee cord stretches
more than twice its original length.

The jump master (top) makes sure the jumper is safely attached.

How do jump masters (who organize and run bungee jumps) know how long to make the cords? The number and length of the cords depends on the weight of the jumper. A heavier jumper would need stronger but shorter cords, since the cords would stretch more. A lighter jumper could use longer cords, since the cords won't stretch as far. Jump masters carefully weigh each jumper to make sure they use the right cords.

Bungee Running?
Bungee cords are also used in a game sometimes seen at carnivals. No jumping necessary! In this game, people wear a harness around their chest. The harness has bungee cords at the back. The people try to run forward on a bouncy surface as far as they can. Once they reach the end, they hop up . . . and the bungee cords zing them back to where they started!

Once the person is strapped in by an expert, it's time to make the leap. Jumpers are helped to the edge of the platform. First-time jumpers are very nervous, of course. People who have jumped before are more excited. In either case, they look out or down . . . and jump!

People bungee jump in several ways. Most do a swan dive, much like diving into a pool. They leap out with their arms spread. They fall headfirst toward the ground . . . until the cord tightens and they slow down suddenly. Other jumpers go backward and see the sky above them as they fall. The bat dive is another way to go. The jumper is hung upside down by their feet . . . and dropped head first!

A headfirst dive is the most popular way to make a bungee jump.

This flip is the start of a bouncy ride!

In some places, you can bungee jump in pairs. Two people are strapped to the same, extra-strong cord. They are also tied together at the waist or chest. Then off they go, down and down and down—together!

Expert jumpers can sometimes do twists or flips on the way down. They risk having the cord become tangled, however. But it adds to the thrill for these brave jumpers.

Bungee jumping looks like a simple sport. But it takes expert planning . . . and a lot of guts!

CHAPTER THREE

Up and Down Stories

Most people who bungee jump leap from popular places such as bridges or platforms over the sea. Thousands of jumpers make these leaps each year. Bungee jumps are often found at beachside resorts. They sometimes are part of traveling carnivals or fairs.

Other daring jumpers look to make their marks by bungee jumping from very high places. The island of Macau is off the coast of China. The Macau Tower there stands 1,109 feet (338 m), soaring above the skyline. Atop the tower is the world's highest public bungee jump. Only the very bravest jumpers take the elevator to the top before bouncing off. A.J. Hackett, the New Zealand pioneer, was the first to make the jump in 2005.

The soaring Macau Tower is a popular bungee site.

This mighty bridge in Colorado was the site
of two famous jumping days.

The highest bridge from which people jump is probably the Royal Gorge Bridge. In 2005 and 2007, special events were held there with permission from Colorado. The bridge soars 1,053 feet (321 m) above the Arkansas River. Jumpers there fall for seven or eight seconds before the cords finally slow them down.

Remember the *GoldenEye* jump? Very brave tourists to Switzerland can now make the same jump as in the movie! A special platform takes jumpers out far enough so that they don't crash into the dam on the way down.

It's not just bridges. Some people bungee jump from hot-air balloons or helicopters. One of the longest bungee jumps ever was from a helicopter in 1991. Andrew Salisbury jumped out from 9,000 feet (more than 2,700 m). After bouncing nearly 3,000 of those feet (962 m), he was still high above the water off Mexico. So he unstrapped and fell to earth beneath a parachute!

Some bungee jumps off bridges come with a bonus: a watery landing. Jump masters can predict exactly how much bungee cord to use so that the jumper's head and chest splash into the river below. It's sort of like the world's hardest way to bob for apples.

Splash! After a long fall, this jumper gets a soaking!

Bungee jumpers keep looking for new places to get their thrills.

Bungee jumpers don't just have to go outdoors, either. At the enormous Edmonton Mall in Canada, they have the world's highest indoor bungee jump. You can do some shopping and then bungee about 100 feet (33 m).

Finally, if you're looking for real bungee adventure, head for Chile. A company there offers bungee jumps into the top of a volcano. You jump out of a helicopter hovering over an active volcano in Chile. You plunge toward the lava before bouncing back up . . . you hope.

Glossary

harness—straps and cords worn by a person or animal to which ropes or cords are attached

lianas—long vines often found in jungle areas

nylon—a type of fabric made as a form of plastic

pioneer—a person who is among the first to do something

stunt man—an expert who performs dangerous feats that are filmed for use in a movie

BOOKS

Weird Sports: Throwing and Kicking Sports
By S.B. Watson. Mankato, MN: The Child's World, 2011.
Bungee jumping is not the only wacky sport out there; check out this
sport for some other sports that take daring!

Bungee Jumping: Living on the Edge
By Shaun McFee. New York, NY: PowerKids Press, 2008.
Another look at this amazing sport, with action photos from around
the world.

WEB SITES

For links to learn more about extreme sports: **childsworld.com/links**

Note to Parents, Teachers, and Librarians: We routinely verify our Web
links to make sure they are safe and active sites. So encourage your
readers to check them out!

Index

About the Author

K. C. Kelley is way too chicken to jump off a high place . . . even with a bungee cord! But he does enjoy writing books for young readers. He has written about baseball, football, and soccer, as well as about animals, astronauts, and other cool stuff.